PUFFIN B

A SINGLE

An anthology of Christmas poetry

Christmas is the time of all the year when everyone needs to sing. Feelings of warmth and love, of anticipation, excitement, beauty and blessed mystery, of enchantment, or even of loneliness and disappointment, are so overpowering then that ordinary mortals, who may be as tongue-tied as anything the rest of the year, will read poetry for the sheer pleasure and relief of having their magical, joyous, wondering Christmas feelings expressed.

The poems here were chosen by David Davis, whose voice on radio is well known and loved, and those parents of today who were reared on his programme *Children's Hour* will almost be able to hear him reading them aloud. He says in his introduction, 'I have chosen nothing that did not light a small lamp of happiness inside me when I came across it.' We know truly that his collection will kindle many more treasured lights of Christmas happiness in every home it enters for many years to come.

A SINGLE STAR

An anthology of Christmas poetry
compiled and arranged by
DAVID DAVIS

ILLUSTRATED BY
MARGERY GILL

PUFFIN BOOKS
in association with The Bodley Head

PUFFIN BOOKS

Published by the Penguin Group
27 Wrights Lane, London w8 5TZ, England
Viking Penguin Inc., 40 West 23rd Street, New York, New York 10010, USA
Penguin Books Australia Ltd, Ringwood, Victoria, Australia
Penguin Books Canada Ltd, 2801 John Street, Markham, Ontario, Canada L3R 1B4
Penguin Books (NZ) Ltd, 182–190 Wairau Road, Auckland 10, New Zealand

Penguin Books Ltd, Registered Offices: Harmondsworth, Middlesex, England

This selection first published by The Bodley Head Ltd 1973
Published in Puffin Books 1976
5 7 9 10 8 6

Printed and bound in Great Britain by
Cox & Wyman Ltd, Reading
Set in Monotype Bembo

CONTENTS

5

5. CHRISTMAS MORNING

6. 'MAKE WE MERRY'

CONTENTS

To B.
with all my love

INTRODUCTION

As all anthologists must do, I have tried, in this collection of Christmas poetry, to avoid including the most hackneyed and most obvious. Some of the old favourites are there, of course, but not many, because they can be found in so many other places. And I have tried to make the mixture not quite as before, but a combination of old (some of it very old) and new. Our old friend 'Anon.' (how he differs from 'Trad.' I am never quite sure) plays a big part, but so do poets of our own time, and particularly those of the inter-war and post-war period. It was a great pleasure to find how many of these there were. I once had an aunt who told me she disliked 'modern' music. When I asked her to be more precise, she said, 'Well, dear, Brahms, perhaps?' By that definition I suppose modern poetry might begin with Christina Rossetti! Though what I had in mind were poets of my own time and generation, and that covers not only the earlier part of the present century, but also the poetry of the fifties, sixties, and seventies. Some names will occur again and again, and I make no apology for it. They are those for whom children and Christmas were always living realities: I think particularly of Walter de la Mare, and Eleanor Farjeon. But what splendid treasures there are in some of the other drawers. It is difficult, and perhaps a little invidious, to particularize. I have included nothing that did not light a small lamp of happiness inside me when I came across it. But I find deeply moving such things as James Kirkup's 'The Eve of Christmas': Ian Serraillier's 'The Mayor and the Simpleton': and Leonard Clark's two poems: 'Singing in the Streets', and 'Bells ringing'. 'The Computer's First Christmas Card' always makes me laugh. And I do feel, looking back on some, though not by any means all, of my own childhood Christmases, a certain wry sympathy with Elizabeth Jennings' poem which I have called 'Afterthought'; and fourteen-year-old Thomas Boyle's 'Christmas to me was Snow'. Even the best of Christmases sometimes have their snags.

The plan of the anthology is based partly on time, partly on the Gospel accounts of the birth of Jesus Christ. (Are we nowadays in danger of forgetting just what it is we are celebrating? I sometimes wonder.) It begins with the wonderful season of Anticipation, which I have associated, as we do in the northern hemisphere, in the best Christmas-card tradition, even if in defiance of reality, with winter and snow. Then, what for me has always been the most magical moment of all, the rapt waiting-time of Christmas Eve, leading on to the very Key of the Kingdom: Bethlehem, and the Stable, with the homage of the Shepherds. Christmas Day itself I have divided, like Julius Caesar, into three parts: morning, afternoon, and night; the afternoon, ('Make We Merry'), being given over to feasting and revelry, riddles, games, and the telling of tales. After the quiet farewell of Christmas Night, we look forward to Epiphany and After.

A word about the titles at the head of each poem: sometimes they are my own invention, intended to show the place they had in my own mind when I was choosing them. Occasionally I have kept the original title, when there was one. Often, it seemed better simply to quote the opening line.

Finally, who is it all aimed at? Children, I think, as far as possible: either to read to themselves, or to be read to. Some of it may be above their heads, but not all. One can never tell.

David Davis

1
Prologue

THE CHILDREN'S CAROL

Here we come again, again, and here we come again,
Christmas is a single pearl swinging on a chain,
Christmas is a single flower in a barren wood,
Christmas is a single sail on the salty flood,
Christmas is a single star in the empty sky,
Christmas is a single song sung for charity.
Here we come again, again, to sing to you again,
Give a single penny that we may not sing in vain.

ELEANOR FARJEON

2
'Christmas Almost Come'

SNOW'S FALL'N DEEP

Now all the roads to London Town
Are windy-white with snow;
There's shouting and cursing,
And snortings to and fro;
But when night hangs her hundred lamps,

And the snickering frost-fires creep,
Then still, O; dale and hill, O;
Snow's fall'n deep.
Then still, O; dale and hill, O;
Snow's fall'n deep.
The carter cracks his leathery whip;
The ostler shouts Gee-whoa;
The farm dog grunts and sniffs and snuffs;
Bleat sheep; and cattle blow;
Soon Moll and Nan in dream are laid;
And snoring Dick's asleep;
Then still, O; dale and hill, O;
Snow's fall'n deep.
Then still, O; dale and hill, O;
Snow's fall'n deep.

WALTER DE LA MARE

MERRY CHRISTMAS

Christmas comes! He comes, he comes,
Ushered with a rain of plums;
Hollies in the window greet him;
Schools come driving post to meet him,
Gifts precede him, bells proclaim him,
Every mouth delights to name him;
Wet, and cold, and wind, and dark,
Make him but the warmer mark;
And yet he comes not one-embodied,
Universal's the blithe godhead,
And in every festal house
Presence hath ubiquitous.
Curtains, those snug room-enfolders,
Hang upon his million shoulders,
And he has a million eyes
Of fire, and eats a million pies,
And is very merry and wise;
Very wise and very merry,
And loves a kiss beneath the berry.

FROM *Christmas*, LEIGH HUNT

CHRISTMAS IS COMING

Christmas is coming,
  The geese are getting fat,
Please to put a penny
  In the old man's hat.
If you haven't got a penny,
  A ha'penny will do;
If you haven't got a ha'penny,
  Then God bless you!

St Thomas's Day is past and gone,
And Christmas almost come,
    Maidens arise,
    And make your pies,
And save young Bobby some.

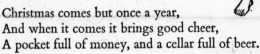

Christmas comes but once a year,
And when it comes it brings good cheer,
A pocket full of money, and a cellar full of beer.

ANON.

15

THE COMPUTER'S FIRST CHRISTMAS CARD

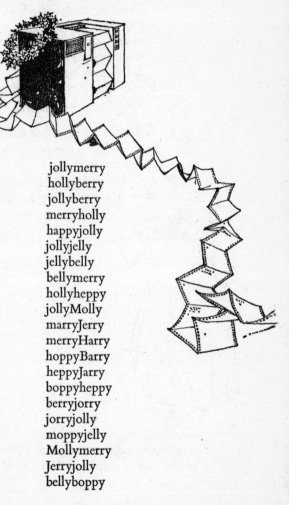

jollymerry
hollyberry
jollyberry
merryholly
happyjolly
jollyjelly
jellybelly
bellymerry
hollyheppy
jollyMolly
marryJerry
merryHarry
hoppyBarry
heppyJarry
boppyheppy
berryjorry
jorryjolly
moppyjelly
Mollymerry
Jerryjolly
bellyboppy

'CHRISTMAS ALMOST COME'

jorryhoppy
hollymoppy
Barrymerry
Jarryhappy
happyboppy
boppyjolly
jollymerry
merrymerry
merrymerry
merryChris
ammerryasa
Chrismerry
as M E R R Y C H R
Y S A N T H E M U M

EDWIN MORGAN

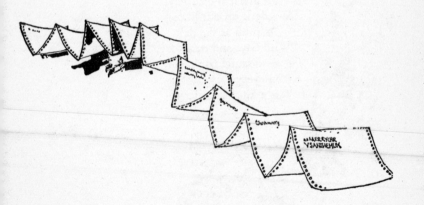

WELCOME YULE

Now, thrice welcome Christmas,
  Which brings us good cheer,
Minced pies and plum porridge,
  Good ale and strong beer;
With pig, goose, and capon,
  The best that can be,
So well doth the weather
  And our stomachs agree.

Observe how the chimneys
  Do smoke all about,
The cooks are providing
  For dinner no doubt;
But those on whose tables
  No victuals appear,
O may they keep Lent
  All the rest of the year!

With holly and ivy
  So green and so gay,
We deck up our houses
  As fresh as the day.
With bays and rosemary,
  And laurel complete;
And everyone now
  Is a king in conceit.

GEORGE WITHER

WINTER

Green Mistletoe!
Oh, I remember now
A dell of snow,
Frost on the bough;
None there but I:
Snow, snow, and a wintry sky.

None there but I,
And footprints one by one,
Zigzaggedly,
Where I had run;
Where shrill and powdery
A robin sat in the tree.

And he whistled sweet;
And I in the crusted snow
With snow-clubbed feet
Jigged to and fro,
Till, from the day,
The rose-light ebbed away.

And the robin flew
Into the air, the air,
The white mist through;
And small and rare
The night-frost fell
Into the calm and misty dell.

And the dusk gathered low,
And the silver moon and stars
On the frozen snow
Drew taper bars,
Kindled winking fires
In the hooded briers.

And the sprawling Bear
Growled deep in the sky;
And Orion's hair
Streamed sparkling by:
But the North sighed low:
'*Snow, snow, more snow!*'

WALTER DE LA MARE

THE ENDING OF THE YEAR

When trees did show no leaves,
   And grass no daisies had,
And fields had lost their sheaves,
   And streams in ice were clad,
And day of light was shorn,
   And wind had got a spear,
Iesus Christ was born
   In the ending of the year.

Like green leaves when they grow,
   He shall for comfort be;
Like life in streams shall flow,
   For running water He;
He shall raise hope like corn
   For barren fields to bear,
And therefore He was born
   In the ending of the year.

Like daisies to the grass,
   His innocence He'll bring;
In keenest winds that pass
   His flowering love shall spring;
The rising of the morn
   At midnight shall appear,
Whenever Christ is born
   In the ending of the year.

ELEANOR FARJEON

3
Christmas Eve

ON CHRISTMAS EVE

On Christmas Eve I turned the spit,
I burnt my fingers, I feel it yet;
The little cock sparrow flew over the table,
The pot began to play with the ladle.

ANON.

SINGING IN THE STREETS

I had almost forgotten the singing in the streets,
Snow piled up by the houses, drifting
Underneath the door into the warm room,
Firelight, lamplight, the little lame cat
Dreaming in soft sleep on the hearth, mother dozing,
Waiting for Christmas to come, the boys and me
Trudging over blanket fields waving lanterns to the sky.
I had almost forgotten the smell, the feel of it all,
The coming back home, with girls laughing like stars,
Their cheeks, holly berries, me kissing one,
Silent-tongued, soberly, by the long church wall;
Then back to the kitchen table, supper on the white cloth,
Cheese, bread, the home-made wine:
Symbols of the Night's joy, a holy feast.
And I wonder now, years gone, mother gone,
The boys and girls scattered, drifted away with the snow-
    flakes,
Lamplight done, firelight over,
If the sounds of our singing in the streets are still there,
Those old tunes, still praising:
And now, a life-time of Decembers away from it all,
A branch of remembering holly spears my cheeks,
And I think it may be so;
Yes, I believe it may be so.

LEONARD CLARK

CAROL OF THE FIELD MICE

Villagers all, this frosty tide,
Let your doors swing open wide,
Though wind may follow, and snow beside,
Yet draw us in by your fire to bide,
   Joy shall be yours in the morning!

Here we stand in the cold and the sleet,
Blowing fingers and stamping feet,
Come from far away you to greet –
You by the fire and we in the street –
   Bidding you joy in the morning!

For ere one half of the night was gone,
Sudden a star has led us on,
Raining bliss and benison –
Bliss tomorrow and more anon,
  Joy for every morning!

Goodman Joseph toiled through the snow –
Saw the star o'er a stable low;
Mary she might not further go –
Welcome thatch, and litter below!
  Joy was hers in the morning!

And then they heard the angels tell
'Who were the first to cry Nowell?
Animals all, as it befell,
In the stable where they did dwell!
  Joy shall be theirs in the morning!'

KENNETH GRAHAME

A CAROL

Our Lord who did the Ox command
  To kneel to Judah's King,
He binds His frost upon the land
  To ripen it for Spring –
To ripen it for Spring, good sirs,
  According to His Word;
Which well must be as ye can see –
  And who shall judge the Lord?

When we poor fenmen skate the ice
  Or shiver on the wold,
We hear the cry of a single tree

That breaks her heart in the cold –
That breaks her heart in the cold, good sirs,
    And rendeth by the board;
Which well must be as ye can see –
    And who shall judge the Lord?

Her wood is crazed and little worth
    Excepting as to burn,
That we may warm and make our mirth
    Until the Spring return –
Until the Spring return, good sirs,
    When people walk abroad;
Which well must be as ye can see –
    And who shall judge the Lord?

God bless the master of this house,
    And all who sleep therein!
And guard the fens from pirate folk,
    And keep us all from sin,
To walk in honesty, good sirs,
    Of thought and deed and word!
Which shall befriend our latter end . . .
    And who shall judge the Lord?

RUDYARD KIPLING

EDDI'S SERVICE
(A.D. 687)

Eddi, priest of St Wilfrid
   In the chapel at Manhood End,
Ordered a midnight service
   For such as cared to attend.

But the Saxons were keeping Christmas,
   And the night was stormy as well.
Nobody came to service,
   Though Eddi rang the bell.

'Wicked weather for walking,'
   Said Eddi of Manhood End.
'But I must go on with the service
   For such as care to attend.'

The altar-lamps were lighted, –
   An old marsh-donkey came,
Bold as a guest invited,
   And stared at the guttering flame.

The storm beat on at the windows,
   The water splashed on the floor,
And a wet, yoke-weary bullock
   Pushed in through the open door.

'How do I know what is greatest,
　　How do I know what is least?
That is my Father's business,'
　　Said Eddi, Wilfrid's priest.

'But – three are gathered together –
　　Listen to me and attend.
I bring good news, my brethren!'
　　Said Eddi, of Manhood End.

And he told the Ox of a manger,
　　And a stall in Bethlehem,
And he spoke to the Ass of a Rider
　　That rode to Jerusalem.

They steamed and dripped in the chancel,
　　They listened and never stirred,
While, just as though they were Bishops,
　　Eddi preached them The Word.

Till the gale blew off on the marshes
　　And the windows showed the day,
And the Ox and the Ass together
　　Wheeled and clattered away.

And when the Saxons mocked him,
　　Said Eddi of Manhood End,
'I dare not shut His chapel
　　On such as care to attend.'

RUDYARD KIPLING

THE EVE OF CHRISTMAS

It was the evening before the night
That Jesus turned from dark to light.

Joseph was walking round and round,
And yet he moved not on the ground.

He looked into the heavens, and saw
The pole stood silent, star on star.

He looked into the forest: there
The leaves hung dead upon the air.

He looked into the sea, and found
It frozen, and the lively fishes bound.

And in the sky, the birds that sang
Not in feathered clouds did hang.

Said Joseph: 'What is this silence all?'
An angel spoke: 'It is no thrall,

But is a sign of great delight:
The Prince of Love is born this night.'

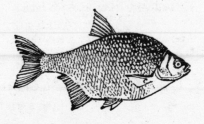

And Joseph said: 'Where may I find
This wonder?' – 'He is all mankind,

Look, he is both farthest, nearest,
Highest and lowest, of all men the dearest.'

Then Joseph moved, and found the stars
Moved with him, and the evergreen airs,

The birds went flying, and the main
Flowed with its fishes once again.

And everywhere they went, they cried:
'Love lives, when all had died!'

In Excelsis Gloria!

JAMES KIRKUP

BELLS RINGING

I heard bells ringing
Suddenly all together, one wild, intricate figure,
A mixture of wonder and praise
Climbing the winter-winged air in December.
Norwich, Gloucester, Salisbury, combined with York
To shake Worcester and Paul's into the old discovery
Made frost-fresh again.
I heard these rocketing and wound-remembering chimes
Running their blessed counterpoint
Round the mazes of my mind,
And felt their message brimming over with love,
Watering my cold heart,
Until, as over all England hundreds of towers trembled
Beneath the force of Christmas rolling out,
I knew, as shepherds and magi knew,
That all sounds had been turned into one sound,
And a single golden bell,
Repeating, as knees bowed, the name EMMANUEL.

LEONARD CLARK

4
Bethlehem

O LITTLE TOWN

O little town of Bethlehem
  How still we see thee lie!
Above thy deep and dreamless sleep
  The silent stars go by.
Yet in thy dark streets shineth

BETHLEHEM

The everlasting light;
The hopes and fears of all the years
Are met in thee tonight.

O morning stars, together
Proclaim the holy birth,
And praises sing to God the King,
And peace to men on earth;
For Christ is born of Mary;
And, gathered all above,
While mortals sleep, the angels keep
Their watch of wondering love.

How silently, how silently,
The wondrous gift is given!
So God imparts to human hearts
The blessings of his heaven.

No ear may hear his coming;
  But in this world of sin,
Where meek souls will receive him, still
  The dear Christ enters in.

Where children pure and happy
  Pray to the blessèd Child,
Where misery cries out to thee,
  Son of the mother mild:
Where charity stands watching
  And faith holds wide the door,
The dark night wakes, the glory breaks,
  And Christmas comes once more.

O holy Child of Bethlehem,
  Descend to us, we pray;
Cast out our sin, and enter in,
  Be born in us today.
We hear the Christmas Angels
  The great glad tidings tell:
O come to us, abide with us,
  Our Lord Emmanuel.

BISHOP PHILLIPS BROOKS

HOW FAR TO BETHLEHEM?

How far is it to Bethlehem?
Not very far.
Shall we find the stable-room
Lit by a star?

Can we see the little child,

Is He within?
If we lift the wooden latch
May we go in?

May we stroke the creatures there,
Ox, ass and sheep?
May we peep like them and see
Jesus asleep?

If we touch His tiny hand
Will He awake?
Will He know we've come so far
Just for His sake?

Great kings have precious gifts,
And we have naught;
Little smiles and little tears
Are all we brought.

For all weary children
Mary must weep.
Here on His bed of straw
Sleep, children, sleep.

God in His mother's arms,
Babes in the byre
Sleep as they sleep who find
Their heart's desire.

FRANCES CHESTERTON

A SINGING IN THE AIR

A snowy field! A stable piled
With straw! A donkey's sleepy pow!
A Mother beaming on a Child!
A Manger, and a munching cow!
– These we all remember now –
And airy voices, heard afar!
And three Magicians, and a Star!

Two thousand times of snow declare
That on the Christmas of the year
There is a singing in the air;
And all who listen for it hear
A fairy chime, a seraph strain,
Telling He is born again,
– That all we love is born again.

FROM *Christmas at Freelands,*
JAMES STEPHENS

AN ODE
ON THE BIRTH
OF OUR
SAVIOUR

In numbers, and but these few,
I sing thy birth, O Jesu!
Thou pretty baby, born here,
With superabundant scorn here,
Who for thy princely port here,
   Hadst for thy place
    Of birth, a base
Out-stable for thy court here.

Instead of neat enclosures
Of interwoven osiers;
Instead of fragrant posies
Of daffodils, and roses:
Thy cradle, kingly stranger,
   As gospel tells,
    Was nothing else
But here a homely manger.

But we with silks, (not crewels)
With sundry precious jewels,
And lily-work will dress thee;
And, as we dispossess thee
Of clouts, we'll make a chamber,
  Sweet babe, for thee,
    Of ivory,
And plastered round with amber.

The Jews, they did disdain thee,
But we will entertain thee
With glories to await here
Upon thy princely state here,
And, more for love than pity,
  From year to year
    We'll make thee here
A free-born of our city.

ROBERT HERRICK

BEHOLD A SIMPLE TENDER BABE

Behold, a simple tender babe
  In freezing winter night
In homely manger trembling lies:
  Alas, a piteous sight!

The inns are full; no man will yield
  This little pilgrim bed;
But forced he is with simple beasts
  In crib to shroud his head.

Despise him not for lying there;
  First what he is inquire:

An orient pearl is often found
  In depth of dirty mire.

Weigh not his crib, his wooden dish,
  Nor beasts that by him feed;
Weigh not his mother's poor attire,
  Nor Joseph's simple weed.

This stable is a prince's court,
  This crib his chair of state,
The beasts are parcel of his pomp,
  The wooden dish his plate;

The persons in that poor attire
  His royal liveries wear;
The Prince himself is come from heaven,
  This pomp is prizèd there.

With joy approach, O Christian wight,
  Do homage to thy King;
And highly praise his humble pomp,
  Which he from heaven doth bring.

ROBERT SOUTHWELL

LUTE-BOOK LULLABY

Sweet was the song the Virgin sang,
  When she to Bethlehem Judah came
And was delivered of a son,
  That blessèd Jesus hath to name:
    Lulla, lulla, lulla, lulla-by:
    Lulla, lulla, lulla, lulla-by.

'Sweet babe,' sang she, 'my Son,
    And eke a Saviour born,
Who hast vouchsafèd from on high
    To visit us that were forlorn:
        Lalula, lalula, lalula-by.'
'Sweet babe,' sang she,
And rocked him sweetly on her knee.

ANON.

A CHRISTMAS CAROL

The Christ-child lay on Mary's lap,
    His hair was like a light.
(O weary, weary were the world,
    But here is all aright.)

The Christ-child lay on Mary's breast,
    His hair was like a star.
(O stern and cunning are the Kings,
    But here the true hearts are.)

The Christ-child lay on Mary's heart,
  His hair was like a fire.
(O weary, weary, is the world,
  But here the world's desire.)

The Christ-child stood at Mary's knee,
  His hair was like a crown,
And all the flowers looked up at him,
  And all the stars looked down.

G. K. CHESTERTON

CAROL

Sing, happy child, Noël, Noël,
Bright shines Orion's sword
Where every star stands sentinel
And watchful of their Lord.

Sweetly the carol singers speak,
They fill the firelit hall,
Singing of Mary, fair and meek,
And Jesus in the stall.

Hark, happy child, to what they say,
Lock in your heart their song

Lest you should lose it on the way
When every road seems long.

You will recall the spicèd scent
Of leaves where no winds stir,
When gold and frankincense are spent,
And nothing's left but myrrh.

EILUNED LEWIS

LULLABY

Sleep, my baby, the night is coming soon.
Sleep, my baby, the day has broken down.

Sleep now: let silence come, let the shadows form
A castle of strength for you, a fortress of calm.

You are so small, sleep will come with ease.
Hush, now, be still now, join the silences.

ELIZABETH JENNINGS

THE SHEPHERDS

From far away we come to you,
  The snow in the street and the wind on the door,
To tell of great tidings strange and true.
  Minstrels and maids stand forth on the floor:
    From far away we come to you,
    To tell of great tidings strange and true,

For as we wandered far and wide,
  The snow in the street and the wind on the door,
What hap do you deem there should us betide?
  Minstrels and maids stand forth on the floor:
    From far away we come to you,
    To tell of great tidings strange and true.

Under a bent when the night was deep,
  The snow in the street and the wind on the door,
There lay three shepherds tending their sheep:
  Minstrels and maids stand forth on the floor:
    From far away we come to you,
    To tell of great tidings strange and true.

'O ye shepherds, what have ye seen,
  The snow in the street and the wind on the door,
To slay your sorrow and heal your teen?'
  Minstrels and maids stand forth on the floor:
    From far away we come to you,
    To tell of great tidings strange and true.

'In an ox-stall this night we saw
  The snow in the street and the wind on the door,
A babe and a maid without a flaw:
    Minstrels and maids stand forth on the floor:
      From far away we come to you,
        To tell of great tidings strange and true.

'There was an old man there beside:
  The snow in the street and the wind on the door,
His hair was white and his hood was wide:
    Minstrels and maids stand forth on the floor:
      From far away we come to you,
        To tell of great tidings strange and true.

'And as we gazed this thing upon,
  The snow in the street and the wind on the door,
Those twain knelt down to the little one.'
    Minstrels and maids stand forth on the floor:
      From far away we come to you,
        To tell of great tidings strange and true.

'And a marvellous song we straight did hear,
  The snow in the street and the wind on the door,
That slew our sorrow and healed our care.'
    Minstrels and maids stand forth on the floor:
      From far away we come to you,
        To tell of great tidings strange and true.

News of a fair and a marvellous thing,
  The snow in the street and the wind on the door,
Nowell, nowell, nowell, we sing!
    Minstrels and maids stand forth on the floor:
      From far away we come to you,
        To tell of great tidings strange and true.

WILLIAM MORRIS

THE MAYOR AND THE SIMPLETON

They followed the Star to Bethlehem –
Boolo the baker, Barleycorn the farmer,
old Darby and Joan, a small boy Peter, and
a simpleton whose name was Innocent.
Over the snowfields and the frozen rutted lanes
they followed the Star to Bethlehem.

Innocent stood at the stable door
and watched them enter. A flower
stuck out of his yellow hair; his mouth gaped open
like a drawer that wouldn't shut.
He beamed upon the child where he lay
among the oxen, in swaddling clothes in the hay,
his blue eyes shining steady as the Star overhead;
beside him old Joseph and
Mary his mother, smiling.
                    Innocent was delighted.

They brought gifts with them – Boolo, some fresh crusty
   loaves
(warm from the baking) which he laid
at the feet of the infant Jesus, kneeling
in all humility.

                    Innocent was delighted.

Barleycorn brought two baskets – one with a dozen eggs,
the other with two chickens – which he laid
at the feet of the infant Jesus, kneeling
in all humility.

                    Innocent was delighted.

Darby and Joan brought apples and pears from their garden,
wrapped in her apron and stuffed
in the pockets of his trousers; the little boy
a pot of geraniums – he had grown them himself.
And they laid them
at the feet of the infant Jesus, kneeling
in all humility.

                    Innocent was delighted.

The mayor rolled up in his coach with a jingle of bells
and a great to-do. He stepped out with a flourish
and fell flat on his face in the snow. His footmen
picked him up and opened his splendid
crimson umbrella. Then he strutted to the door,
while the white flakes floated down
and covered it with spots. He was proud of his umbrella
and didn't mean to give it away.

Shaking the snow off on to the stable floor,
the mayor peered down at the child where he lay
among the oxen, in swaddling clothes in the hay,
his blue eyes shining steady as the Star overhead,
beside him old Joseph and
Mary his mother, smiling.

       Innocent was puzzled.

And the mayor said: 'On this important occasion
each must take a share in the general thanksgiving.
Hence the humble gifts – the very humble gifts –
which I see before me. My own contribution
is something special – a speech. I made it up myself and I'm sure
you'll all like it. Ahem. Pray silence for the mayor.'

 'Moo, moo,' said the oxen.

         'My fellow citizens,
the happy event I refer to – in which we all rejoice –
has caused a considerable stir
in the parish –'

    '– in the whole world,' said a voice.

48

Who spoke? Could it be Innocent, always so shy,
timid as a butterfly, frightened
as a sparrow with a broken wing? Yes, it was he.
Now God had made him bold.

   'I fear I must start again,' said the mayor.
'My fellow citizens, in the name of the people of this parish
I am proud to welcome one
who promises so well –'
                     '– He is the Son of Heaven,'
said Innocent.

              The mayor took no notice.
'I prophesy a fine future for him,
almost – you might say – spectacular.
He'll do us all credit. At the same time I salute in particular
the child's mother, the poor woman who –'
   '– She is not poor but the richest, most radiant
of mothers.'
   'Simpleton, how dare you interrupt!'
snapped the mayor.

But God, who loves the humble, heard him not.
He made him listen, giving Innocent the words:
'Mr Mayor, you don't understand. This birth
is no local event. The child is Jesus,
King of kings and Lord of lords.
A stable is his place and poverty his dwelling-place –
yet he has come to save the world. No speech
is worthy of him –'

       'Tush!' said the mayor.

'I took a lot of trouble. It's a rare
and precious gift, my speech – and now
I can't get a word in edgeways.'

'Rare and precious, did you say? Hear what the child
has brought to *us* – peace on earth, goodwill toward men.
O truly rare and precious gift!'
    'Peace on earth,' said the neighbours,
'goodwill toward men. O truly rare
and precious gift!' They knelt in humility,
in gratitude to the child who lay
among the oxen, in swaddling clothes in the hay,
his blue eyes shining steady as the Star overhead,
beside him old Joseph and
Mary his mother, smiling.

The mayor was silent. God gave the simpleton
no more to say. Now
like a frightened bird
over the snowfields and the frozen rutted lanes
he fluttered away. Always, as before, a flower
stuck out of his yellow hair; his mouth gaped open
like a drawer that wouldn't shut.
He never spoke out like that again.

As for the mayor, he didn't finish his speech.
He called for his coach and drove off, frowning,
much troubled. For a little while
he thought of what the simpleton had said
But he soon forgot all about it, having
important business to attend to in town.

IAN SERRAILLIER

THE KEY OF THE KINGDOM

This is the key of the kingdom:
In that kingdom is a city,
In that city is a town,
In that town there is a street,
In that street there winds a lane,
In that lane there is a yard,
In that yard there is a house,
In that house there waits a room,
In that room there is a bed,
On that bed there is a basket.
   A basket of flowers.

Flowers in the basket,
Basket on the bed,
Bed in the chamber,
Chamber in the house,
House in the weedy yard,
Yard in the winding lane,
Lane in the broad street,
Street in the high town,
Town in the city,
City in the kingdom:
   This is the key of the kingdom.

ANON.

THE INNKEEPER'S WIFE

I love this byre. Shadows are kindly here.
The light is flecked with travelling stars of dust.
So quiet it seems after the inn-clamour,
Scraping of fiddles and the stamping feet.

Only the cows, each in her patient box,
Turn their slow eyes, as we and the sunlight enter,
Their slowly rhythmic mouths.
                              'That is the stall,
 Carpenter. You see it's too far gone
For patching or repatching. My husband made it,
And he's been gone these dozen years and more . . .'
Strange how this lifeless thing, degraded wood
Split from the tree and nailed and crucified
To make a wall, outlives the mastering hand
That struck it down, the warm firm hand
That touched my body with its wandering love.
'No, let the fire take them. Strip every board
And make a new beginning. Too many memories lurk
Like worms in this old wood. That piece you're holding –
That patch of grain with the giant's thumbprint --
I stared at it a full hour when he died:
Its grooves are down my mind. And that board there
Baring its knot-hole like a missing jig-saw –
I remember another hand along its rim.
No, not my husband's, and why I should remember
I cannot say. It was a night in winter.
Our house was full, tight-packed as salted herrings –
So full, they said, we had to hold our breaths
To close the door and shut the night-air out!
And then two travellers came. They stood outside
Across the threshold, half in the ring of light
And half beyond it. I would have let them in
Despite the crowding – the woman was past her time –
But I'd no mind to argue with my husband,
The flagon in my hand and half the inn
Still clamouring for wine. But when trade slackened,
And all our guests had sung themselves to bed
Or told the floor their troubles, I came out here
Where he had lodged them. The man was standing

As you are now, his hand smoothing that board. –
He was a carpenter, I heard them say.
She rested on the straw, and on her arm
A child was lying. None of your creased-faced brats
Squalling their lungs out. Just lying there
As calm as a new-dropped calf – his eyes wide open,
And gazing round as if the world he saw
In the chaff-strewn light of the stable lantern
Was something beautiful and new and strange.
Ah well, he'll have learnt different now, I reckon,
Wherever he is. And why I should recall
A scene like that, when times I would remember
Have passed beyond reliving, I cannot think.
It's a trick you're served by old possessions:
They have their memories too – too many memories.
Well, I must go in. There are meals to serve.
Join us there, Carpenter, when you've had enough
Of cattle-company. The world is a sad place,
But wine and music blunt the truth of it.'

CLIVE SANSOM

5
Christmas Morning

WELCOME TO HEAVEN'S KING

Welcome be Thou, Heaven's King,
Welcome, born in one morning,
Welcome, for Him we shall sing,
   Welcome, Yule!

                              ANON.

LITTLE CHRIST JESUS

Now every Child that dwells on earth,
Stand up, stand up and sing:
The passing night has given birth
Unto the children's King.
Sing sweet as the flute,
Sing clear as the horn,
Sing joy of the Children,
Come Christmas the morn:
> *Little Christ Jesus*
> *Our brother is born.*

Now every star that dwells in sky,
Look down with shining eyes:
The night has dropped in passing by
A Star from Paradise.
Sing sweet as the flute,
Sing clear as the horn,
Sing joy of the Stars,
Come Christmas the morn:
> *Little Christ Jesus*
> *Our brother is born.*

Now every Beast that crops in field,
Breathe sweetly and adore:
The night has brought the richest yield
That ever the harvest bore.
Sing sweet as the flute,
Sing clear as the horn,
Sing joy of the Creatures,
Come Christmas the morn:
> *Little Christ Jesus*
> *Our brother is born.*

Now every Bird that flies in air,
Sing, raven, lark and dove:
The night has brooded on her lair
And fledged the Bird of love.
Sing sweet as the flute,
Sing clear as the horn,
Sing joy of the Birds,
Come Christmas the morn:
    Little Christ Jesus
    Our brother is born.

Now all the Angels of the Lord,
Rise up on Christmas Even:
The passing night will hear the Word
That is the voice of Heaven.
Sing sweet as the flute,
Sing clear as the horn,
Sing joy of the Angels,
Come Christmas the morn:
    Little Christ Jesus
    Our brother is born.

ELEANOR FARJEON

IT WAS ON CHRISTMAS DAY

It was on Christmas Day,
And all in the morning,
Our Saviour was born,
And our heavenly King:
And was not this a joyful thing?
And sweet Jesus they called him by name.

ANON.

AS I SAT ON A SUNNY BANK

As I sat on a sunny bank
On Christmas day in the morning,
I saw three ships come sailing by
On Christmas day in the morning.
And who do you think were in those ships
But Joseph and his fair lady:
He did whistle and she did sing,
And all the bells on earth did ring
For joy our Saviour He was born
On Christmas day in the morning.

ANON.

BEFORE THE PALING OF THE STARS

Before the paling of the stars,
Before the winter morn,
Before the earliest cock-crow,
Jesus Christ was born:
Born in a stable,
Cradled in a manger,
In the world His hands had made
Born a stranger.

Priest and King lay fast asleep
   In Jerusalem;
Young and old lay fast asleep
   In crowded Bethlehem;
Saint and Angel, ox and ass,
   Kept a watch together,
   Before the Christmas daybreak
   In the winter weather.

Jesus on His Mother's breast
   In the stable cold,
Spotless Lamb of God was He,
   Shepherd of the fold:
Let us kneel with Mary Maid,
   With Joseph bent and hoary,
With Saint and Angel, ox and ass,
   To hail the King of Glory.

CHRISTINA ROSSETTI

AFTERTHOUGHT

For weeks before it comes I feel excited, yet when it
At last arrives, things all go wrong:
My thoughts don't seem to fit.

I've planned what I'll give everyone and what they'll give
   to me,
And then on Christmas morning all
The presents seem to be

Useless and tarnished. I have dreamt that everything would
   come
To life – presents and people too.
Instead of that, I'm dumb,

And people say, 'How horrid! What a sulky little boy!'
And they are right. I *can't* seem pleased.
The lovely shining toy

I wanted so much when I saw it in a magazine
Seems pointless now. And Christmas too
No longer seems to mean

The hush, the star, the baby, people being kind again.
The bells are rung, sledges are drawn,
And peace on earth for men.

ELIZABETH JENNINGS

6
'Make We Merry'

MAKE WE MERRY

Make we merry, both more and less,
For now is the time of Christemas.

Let no man come into this hall,
Nor groom, nor page, not yet marshall,
But that some sport he bring withal.

If that he say he cannot sing,
Some other sport then let him bring,
That it may please at this feasting.

If he say he naught can do,
Then, for my love, ask him no mo'
But to the stocks then let him go.

Make we merry, both more and less,
For now is the time of Christemas.

ANON.

OUR JOYFULL'ST FEAST

So, now is come our joyfull'st feast;
  Let every man be jolly.
Each room with ivy-leaves is dressed,
  And every post with holly.
Though some churls at our mirth repine,
Round your foreheads garlands twine,
Drown sorrow in a cup of wine,
  And let us all be merry.

Now, all our neighbours' chimneys smoke,
  And Christmas blocks are burning;
Their ovens, they with baked meats choke,
  And all their spits are turning.

Without the door let sorrow lie,
And if for cold it hap to die,
We'll bury it in a Christmas pie,
    And evermore be merry.

FROM *A Christmas Carol*, GEORGE WITHER

WASSAIL!

Wassail, wassail, all over the town!
Our toast it is white, and our ale it is brown,
Our bowl it is made of the white maple tree;
With the wassailing bowl we'll drink to thee!

So here is to Cherry and to his right cheek,
Pray God send our master a good piece of beef,
And a good piece of beef that may we all see;
With the wassailing bowl we'll drink to thee!

And here is to Dobbin and to his right eye,
Pray God send our master a good Christmas pie,
And a good Christmas pie that may we all see;
With our wassailing bowl we'll drink to thee!

So here is to Broad May and to her broad horn,
May God send our master a good crop of corn,
And a good crop of corn that may we all see;
With the wassailing bowl we'll drink to thee!

And here is to Fill-Pail and to her left ear,
Pray God send our master a happy New Year,
And a happy New Year as e'er he did see;
With our wassailing bowl we'll drink to thee!

And here is to Colly and to her long tail,
Pray God send our master he never may fail
A bowl of strong beer; I pray you draw near,
And our jolly wassail it's then you shall hear!

Come, butler, come fill us a bowl of the best,
Then we hope that your soul in heaven may rest:
But if you do draw us a bowl of the small,
Then down shall go butler, bowl and all.

Then here's to the maid in the lily-white smock,
Who tripped to the door and slipped back the lock!
Who tripped to the door and pulled back the pin,
For to let these jolly wassailers in!

ANON.

SOME CHRISTMAS RIDDLES

Flour of England, fruit of Spain,
Met together in a shower of rain;
Put in a bag, tied round with a string;
If you tell me this riddle,
I'll give you a ring.
(*Plum pudding*)

I'm called by the name of a man,
Yet am as little as a mouse;
When winter comes I love to be
With my red target near the house.
(*A robin*)

Highty, tighty, paradighty,
Clothed all in green,
The king could not read it,
No more could the queen;
They sent for the wise men
From out of the East,
Who said it had horns,
But was not a beast.

(A holly-leaf)

ANON.

SNAPDRAGON

Here he comes with flaming bowl,
Don't he mean to take his toll,
  Snip! Snap! Dragon.
Take care you don't take too much,
Be not greedy in your clutch,
  Snip! Snap! Dragon.

With his blue and lapping tongue
Many of you will be stung,
  Snip! Snap! Dragon.
For he snaps at all that comes
Snatching at his feast of plums,
  Snip! Snap! Dragon.

But old Christmas makes him come,
Though he looks so fee! fo! fum!
    Snip! Snap! Dragon.
Don't 'ee fear him, but be bold,
Out he goes, his flames are cold,
    Snip! Snap! Dragon.

ANON.

A SONG FOR ANYONE TO SING

There was a pig went out to dig,
On Chrisimas Day, Chrisimas Day,
There was a pig went out to dig
On Chrisimas Day in the morning.

There was a cow went out to plough,
On Chrisimas Day, Chrisimas Day,
There was a cow went out to plough
On Chrisimas Day in the morning.

There was a doe went out to hoe,
On Chrisimas Day, Chrisimas Day,
There was a doe went out to hoe
On Chrisimas Day in the morning.

There was a drake went out to rake,
On Chrisimas Day, Chrisimas Day,
There was a drake went out to rake
On Chrisimas Day in the morning.

There was a sparrow went out to harrow,
On Chrisimas Day, Chrisimas Day,
There was a sparrow went out to harrow
On Chrisimas Day in the morning.

There was a minnow went out to winnow,
On Chrisimas Day, Chrisimas Day,
There was a minnow went out to winnow
On Chrisimas Day in the morning.

There was a sheep went out to reap,
On Chrisimas Day, Chrisimas Day,
There was a sheep went out to reap
On Chrisimas Day in the morning.

There was a crow went out to sow,
On Chrisimas Day, Chrisimas Day,
There was a crow went out to sow
On Chrisimas Day in the morning.

There was a row went out to mow,
On Chrisimas Day, Chrisimas Day,
There was a row went out to mow
On Chrisimas Day in the morning.

ANON.

GHOST STORY

Bring out the tall tales now that we told
by the fire as the gaslight bubbled like a diver.
Ghosts whooed like owls in the long nights
when I dared not look over my shoulder; animals
lurked in the cubbyhole under the stairs where the
gas meter ticked. And I remember that we went
singing carols once, when there wasn't the shaving
of a moon to light the flying streets. At the end
of a long road was a drive that led to a large
house, and we stumbled up the darkness of the drive
that night, each one of us afraid, each one holding
a stone in his hand in case, and all of us too brave
to say a word. The wind through the trees
made noises as of old and unpleasant and maybe
webfooted men wheezing in caves. We reached
the black bulk of the house.
'What shall we give them? Hark the Herald?'
'No,' Jack said, 'Good King Wenceslas.
I'll count three.'

One, two, three, and we began to sing,
our voices high and seemingly distant in the
snow-felted darkness round the house that
was occupied by nobody we knew. We stood
close together, near the dark door.
'*Good King Wenceslas looked out*
On the Feast of Stephen . . .'
And then a small, dry voice, like the voice
of someone who has not spoken for a long time,
joined our singing: a small dry eggshell voice
from the other side of the door: a small dry voice
through the keyhole. And when we stopped running
we were outside *our* house; the front room was lovely:
balloons floated under the hot-water-bottle-gulping gas;
everything was good again and shone over the town.

'Perhaps it was a ghost,' Jim said.
'Perhaps it was trolls,' Dan said,
who was always reading.

'Let's go in and see if there's any jelly left,'
Jack said. And we did that.

DYLAN THOMAS

CHRISTMAS TO ME WAS SNOW

Christmas to me
was snow
but it never snowed
it always rained
or was sunny.
Once it snowed
and that was Christmas.
But the turkey got burnt
and when you chewed it
Mum said 'Do you like it?'
and you said 'Yes'
and that was her Christmas.
Dad's was a cigar
or an ounce of St Bruno or new slippers.

THOMAS BOYLE (AGED 14)

7
Christmas Night

THIS HOLY NIGHT

God bless your house this holy night,
    And all within it;
God bless the candle that you light
    To midnight's minute:

The board at which you break your bread,
  The cup you drink of:
And as you raise it, the unsaid
  Name that you think of:
The warming fire, the bed of rest,
  The ringing laughter:
These things, and all things else be blest
  From floor to rafter
This holy night, from dark to light,
  Even more than other;
And, if you have no house tonight,
  God bless you, brother.

ELEANOR FARJEON

HOLLY RED AND
MISTLETOE WHITE

Holly red and mistletoe white,
The stars are shining with golden light,
Burning like candles this Holy Night,
Holly red and mistletoe white.

Mistletoe white and holly red,
The doors are shut and the children a-bed,
Fairies at foot and angels at head,
Mistletoe white and holly red.

ALISON UTTLEY

THE FIRST TREE IN
THE GREENWOOD

Now the holly bears a berry as white as the milk,
And Mary bore Jesus, who was wrapped up in silk:
  And Mary bore Jesus Christ,
  Our Saviour for to be,
  And the first tree in the greenwood, it was the holly.

Now the holly bears a berry as green as the grass,
And Mary bore Jesus, who died on the cross:
  And Mary bore Jesus Christ,
  Our Saviour for to be,
  And the first tree in the greenwood, it was the holly.

Now the holly bears a berry as black as the coal,
And Mary bore Jesus, who died for us all:
    And Mary bore Jesus Christ,
    Our Saviour for to be,
    And the first tree in the greenwood, it was the holly.

Now the holly bears a berry, as blood is it red,
Then trust we our Saviour, who rose from the dead:
    And Mary bore Jesus Christ,
    Our Saviour for to be,
    And the first tree in the greenwood, it was the holly.

ANON.

THE CHRISTMAS TREE

Put out the lights now!
Look at the Tree, the rough tree dazzled
In oriole plumes of flame,
Tinselled with twinkling frost fire, tasselled
With stars and moons – the same
That yesterday hid in the spinney and had no fame
Till we put out the lights now.

Hard are the nights now:
The fields at moonrise turn to agate,
Shadows are cold as jet;
In dyke and furrow, in copse and faggot
The frost's tooth is set;
And stars are the sparks whirled out by the north wind's fret
On the flinty nights now.

So feast your eyes now
On mimic star and moon-cold bauble:
Worlds may wither unseen,
But the Christmas Tree is a tree of fable,

CHRISTMAS NIGHT

A phoenix in evergreen,
And the world cannot change or chill what its mysteries mean
To your hearts and eyes now.

The vision dies now
Candle by candle: the tree that embraced it
Returns to its own kind,
To be earthed again and weather as best it
May the frost and the wind.
Children, it too had its hour – you will not mind
If it lives or dies now.

C. DAY LEWIS

YULE LOG

Kindle the Christmas brand, and then
  Till sunset let it burn;
Which quenched, then lay it up again,
  Till Christmas next return.

Part must be kept wherein to tend
  The Christmas log next year,
And where 'tis safely kept, the fiend
  Can do no mischief there.

ROBERT HERRICK

LOVE CAME DOWN
AT CHRISTMAS

Love came down at Christmas,
  Love all lovely, Love Divine;
Love was born at Christmas,
  Star and angels gave the sign.

Worship we the Godhead,
  Love Incarnate, Love Divine;
Worship we our Jesus:
  But wherewith for sacred sign?

78

Love shall be our token,
　　Love be yours and love be mine,
Love to God and all men,
　　Love for plea and gift and sign.

CHRISTINA ROSSETTI

8

Epiphany and After

ALL IN THE MORNING

It was on the Twelfth Day,
And all in the morning,
The Wise Men were led
To our heavenly King;
And was not this a joyful thing?
And sweet Jesus they called him by name.

It was on Twentieth Day,
And all in the morning,
The Wise Men returned
From our heavenly King;
And was not this a joyful thing?
And sweet Jesus they called him by name.

ANON.

THREE KINGS CAME RIDING

Three Kings came riding from far away,
  Melchior and Gaspar and Baltasar;
Three Wise Men out of the East were they,
And they travelled by night and they slept by day,
  For their guide was a beautiful, wonderful star.

The star was so beautiful, large, and clear,
  That all the other stars of the sky
Became a white mist in the atmosphere,
And by this they knew that the coming was near
  Of the Prince foretold in the prophecy.

Three caskets they bore on their saddle-bows,
  Three caskets of gold with golden keys;
Their robes were of crimson silk, with rows
Of bells and pomegranates and furbelows,
  Their turbans like blossoming almond-trees.

And so the Three Kings rode into the West,
  Through the dusk of night, over hill and dell,
And sometimes they nodded, with beard on breast,
And sometimes talked, as they paused to rest,
  With the people they met at some wayside well.

'Of the child that is born,' said Baltasar,
  'Good people, I pray you, tell us the news;
For we in the East have seen his star,
And have ridden fast, and have ridden far,
  To find and worship the King of the Jews.'

And the people answered, 'You ask in vain;
  We know of no king but Herod the Great!'
They thought the Wise Men were men insane,
As they spurred their horses across the plain,
  Like riders in haste, and who cannot wait.

And when they came to Jerusalem,
  Herod the Great, who had heard this thing,
Sent for the Wise Men and questioned them;
And said, 'Go down unto Bethlehem,
  And bring me tidings of this new king.'

So they rode away; and the star stood still,
  The only one in the grey of morn;
Yes, it stopped, it stood still of its own free will,
Right over Bethlehem on the hill,
  The city of David where Christ was born.

And the Three Kings rode through the gate and the guard,
  Through the silent street, till their horses turned
And neighed as they entered the great inn-yard;
But the windows were closed, and the doors were barred,
  And only a light in the stable burned.

And cradled there in the scented hay,
  In the air made sweet by the breath of kine,
The little child in the manger lay,
The child that would be King one day
  Of a kingdom not human but divine.

His mother, Mary of Nazareth,
  Sat watching beside his place of rest,
Watching the even flow of his breath,
For the joy of life and the terror of death
  Were mingled together in her breast.

They laid their offerings at his feet:
  The gold was their tribute to a King,
The frankincense, with its odour sweet,
Was for the Priest, the Paraclete,
  The myrrh for the body's burying.

And the mother wondered and bowed her head,
  And sat as still as a statue of stone;
Her heart was troubled yet comforted,
Remembering what the Angel had said,
  Of an endless reign and of David's throne.

Then the Kings rode out of the city gate,
  With a clatter of hoofs in proud array;
But they went not back to Herod the Great,
For they knew his malice and feared his hate,
  And returned to their homes by another way.

HENRY WADSWORTH LONGFELLOW

THE
STRANGERS

Dim-berried is the mistletoe
With globes of sheenless grey,
The holly mid ten thousand thorns
Smoulders its fires away;
And in the manger Jesu sleeps
  This Christmas Day.

Bull unto bull with hollow throat
Makes echo every hill,
Cold sheep in pastures thick with snow
The air with bleatings fill;
While of his mother's heart this Babe
  Takes His sweet will.

All flowers and butterflies lie hid,
The blackbird and the thrush
Pipe but a little as they flit
Restless from bush to bush;
Even to the robin Gabriel hath
  Cried softly, 'Hush!'

Now night's astir with burning stars
In darkness of the snow;
Burdened with frankincense and myrrh
And gold the Strangers go
Into a dusk where one dim lamp
  Burns faintly, Lo!

No snowdrop yet its small head nods,
In winds of winter drear;
No lark at casement in the sky
Sings matins shrill and clear;
Yet in this frozen mirk the Dawn
    Breathes, Spring is here!

WALTER DE LA MARE

IN A FAR LAND UPON A DAY

In a far land upon a day,
Where never snow did fall,
Three Kings went riding on the way
Bearing presents all.

And one wore red, and one wore gold,
And one was clad in green,
And one was young, and one was old,
And one was in between.

The middle one had human sense,
The young had loving eyes,
The old had much experience,
And all of them were wise.

Choosing no guide by eve and morn
But heaven's starry drifts,
They rode to find the Newly-Born
For whom they carried gifts.

Oh, far away in time they rode
Upon their wanderings,
And still in story goes abroad
The riding of the Kings:

So wise, that in their chosen hour,
As through the world they filed,
They sought not wealth or place or power,
But rode to find a child.

ELEANOR FARJEON

JOURNEY OF THE MAGI

'A cold coming we had of it,
Just the worst time of the year
For a journey, and such a long journey:
The ways deep and the weather sharp,
The very dead of winter.'
And the camels galled, sore-footed, refractory,
Lying down in the melting snow.
There were times we regretted
The summer palaces on slopes, the terraces,
And the silken girls bringing sherbet.
Then the camel men cursing and grumbling

And running away, and wanting their liquor and women,
And the night-fires going out, and the lack of shelters,
And the cities hostile and the towns unfriendly
And the villages dirty and charging high prices:
A hard time we had of it.
At the end we preferred to travel all night,
Sleeping in snatches,
With the voices singing in our ears, saying
That this was all folly.

   Then at dawn we came down to a temperate valley,
Wet, below the snow line, smelling of vegetation;
With a running stream and a water-mill beating the
   darkness,
And three trees on the low sky,
And an old white horse galloped away in the meadow.
Then we came to a tavern with vine-leaves over the lintel,
Six hands at an open door dicing for pieces of silver,
And feet kicking the empty wine-skins.
But there was no information, and so we continued
And arrived at evening, not a moment too soon
Finding the place: it was (you may say) satisfactory.

All this was a long time ago, I remember,
And I would do it again, but set down
This set down
This: were we led all that way for
Birth or Death? There was a Birth, certainly,
We had evidence and no doubt. I had seen birth and death,
But had thought they were different; this Birth was
Hard and bitter agony for us, like Death, our death.
We returned to our places, these Kingdoms,
But no longer at ease here, in the old dispensation,
With an alien people clutching their gods.
I should be glad of another death.

T. S. ELIOT

INNOCENT'S SONG

Who's that knocking on the window,
Who's that standing at the door,
What are all those presents
Lying on the kitchen floor?

Who is the smiling stranger
With hair as white as gin,

What is he doing with the children
And who could have let him in?

Why has he rubies on his fingers,
A cold, cold crown on his head,
Why, when he caws his carol,
Does the salty snow run red?

Why does he ferry my fireside
As a spider on a thread,
His fingers made of fuses
And his tongue of gingerbread?

Why does the world before him
Melt in a million suns,
Why do his yellow, yearning eyes
Burn like saffron buns?

Watch where he comes walking
Out of the Christmas flame,
Dancing, double-talking:

Herod is his name.

CHARLES CAUSLEY

JOSEPH AND JESUS
(from the Spanish)

Said Joseph unto Mary,
  'Be counselled by me:
Fetch your love child from the manger,
  For to Egypt we must flee.'

As Mary went a-riding
 Up the hill out of view,
The ass was much astonished
 How like a dove he flew.

Said Jesus unto Joseph,
 Who his soft cheek did kiss:
'There are thorns in your beard, good sir.
 I askèd not for this.'

Then Joseph brought to Jesus
 Hot paps of white bread
Which, when it burned that pretty mouth,
 Joseph swallowed in his stead.

ROBERT GRAVES

CRYING, MY LITTLE ONE?

Crying, my little one, footsore and weary?
 Fall asleep, pretty one, warm on my shoulder:
I must tramp on through the winter night dreary,
 While the snow falls on me colder and colder.

You are my one, and I have not another;
 Sleep soft, my darling, my trouble and treasure;
Sleep warm and soft in the arms of your mother,
 Dreaming of pretty things, dreaming of pleasure.

CHRISTINA ROSSETTI

9
Epilogue

A CHRISTMAS BLESSING

God bless the master of this house,
  The mistress also,
And all the little children
That round the table go;
And all your kin and kinsfolk,
  That dwell both far and near:
I wish you a Merry Christmas
  And a Happy New Year.

ANON.

INDEX OF FIRST LINES

INDEX OF FIRST LINES

INDEX OF AUTHORS

ACKNOWLEDGMENTS

The editor and publisher wish to thank the following for permission to reprint copyright material included in this anthology:

The *Daily Mirror* for 'Christmas to me' by Thomas Boyle.

The poet and the publisher (represented by David Higham Associates) for 'Innocent's Song' by Charles Causley from *Johnny Alleluia* published by Rupert Hart-Davis.

Miss D. E. Collins (represented by A. P. Watt & Son) for 'How Far is it to Bethlehem?' by Frances Chesterton.

Miss D. E. Collins and Methuen (represented by A. P. Watt & Son) for 'A Christmas Carol' by G. K. Chesterton from *The Collected Poems of G. K. Chesterton.*

The publisher for 'Singing in the Streets' and 'Bells Ringing' from *Singing in the Streets* by Leonard Clark, published by Dennis Dobson.

The Literary Trustees of Walter de la Mare, and the Society of Authors as their representative, for 'Now all the roads', 'Winter', and 'Dimberried is the mistletoe' by Walter de la Mare.

Faber and Faber Ltd for 'Journey of the Magi' by T. S. Eliot from *Collected Poems 1909–1962.*

The Estate of Eleanor Farjeon and the publisher (represented by David Higham Associates) for 'Here we come again', 'When trees did show no leaves', 'Now every child', 'God bless your house' and 'In a Far Land' by Eleanor Farjeon from *Silver Sand and Snow* published by Michael Joseph.

The Estate of Kenneth Grahame (represented by Curtis Brown Ltd, London) and Charles Scribner's Sons, New York, for 'Carol of the Field Mice' ('Villagers all, this frosty tide') from *The Wind in the Willows* by Kenneth Grahame (1908).

The poet (represented by A. P. Watt & Son) for 'Joseph and Jesus' from *Ann at Highwood Hall* by Robert Graves.

Mrs George Bambridge and the publishers (represented by A. P. Watt & Son) for 'A Carol' and 'Eddi's Service' by Rudyard Kipling from *Rewards and Fairies* published by Macmillan & Co.

The poet for 'The Eve of Christmas' by James Kirkup.

The Executors of the Estate of C. Day Lewis and the publisher, together with the Hogarth Press, for 'The Christmas Tree' from *Collected Poems 1954* by C. Day Lewis published by Jonathan Cape Ltd.

The Society of Authors and the poet for 'Sing, happy child' by Eiluned Lewis.

The Edinburgh University Press for 'The Computer's First Christmas Card' by Edwin Morgan.

The poet and the publisher (represented by David Higham Associates) for 'The Innkeeper's Wife' from *The Witnesses* by Clive Sansom, published by Methuen.

The poet for 'The Mayor and the Simpleton' by Ian Serraillier.

Mrs I. Wise, The Macmillan Company of Canada and Macmillan, London and Basingstoke, for 'A Singing in the Air' from 'Christmas at Freelands' by James Stephens.

Macmillan, London and Basingstoke, for 'Lullaby' and 'Afterthought' from *The Secret Brother* by Elizabeth Jennings.

The Trustees for the Copyrights of the late Dylan Thomas, and the publishers, for the extract from *Quite Early One Morning* by Dylan Thomas, published by J. M. Dent & Sons Ltd.

The publishers for 'Holly red and mistletoe white' from *Little Grey Rabbit's Christmas* by Alison Uttley, published by Collins.